WORDS

Every Child Must Hear

Emotional Nourishment for Children of All Ages

Text and photography by
CYNTHIA GOOD

LONGSTREET PRESS
Atlanta, Georgia

Published by
LONGSTREET PRESS, INC.
A subsidiary of Cox Newspapers,
A division of Cox Enterprises, Inc.
2140 Newmarket Parkway
Suite 118
Marietta, GA 30067

Printed in the United States of America

2nd printing 1994

Library of Congress Catalog Card Number: 93-81139

ISBN 1-56352-138-5

This book was printed by Semline Incorporated, Westwood, Massachusetts.

Jacket and book design by Laura McDonald
Cover concept by Elizabeth O'Dowd

Cover art: *"Baby's First Caress," by Mary Cassatt, from the collection of the New Britain Museum of American Art, Connecticut, Harriet Russell Stanley Fund. Photo by E. Irving Blomstrann.*

To my husband, Joey, who taught me
the meaning of love, and to our son, Alden,
whom we get to share it with

CONTENTS

Foreword

—◄O►—

This book offers necessary reminders of what we can do for our children. It encourages us to be conscious of what we communicate to those who are most precious to us. It's a chance to examine the feelings behind our messages and to ask ourselves, "What do we want to say to this child?"

If you saw two strangers and one was a child, the other an adult, and the adult picked up the child, looked into her eyes, held her close and spoke, you could rightly assume, even if you didn't hear the words, that the adult intended to communicate to the little girl a feeling of caring and love.

Such interchanges, for better or for worse, will happen thousands of times in the course of a child's life. Words spoken with the honest intent of strengthening feelings of love will have a lasting benefit as they enable the child to better accept his impulses and express his true self. This child will have an easier time identifying positive purposes and goals and he will gain a sense of self that is strong but not closed off from the environment.

Through these expressions, Cynthia Good promotes the three things required for emotional health: that children feel loved, that they feel important and that they belong.

Such a child can then react to the world in different ways, expressing sadness when appropriate but moving through hard times to renewed and additional happiness. He will emerge as a beautiful, productive and contributing individual with the capacity to develop deep personal bonds in order to one day begin the process of re-creating the universe.

There's an old proverb that says, "A tree shall grow as the twig is bent." This book is a fine seed.

Arthur M. Cohen, Ph.D.
Atlanta, Georgia

Acknowledgments

———◆◇◆———

This book would not have been possible without my family and friends who shared with me their love, support, wisdom and words.

I thank my soul-mate, Joey, and my friends Denise and Mark Connolly, Sara and Armand Harris, Renee and Steve Alterman, Elizabeth O'Dowd, Mary Ganz, Maureen Goldman and Meg Reggie; my news director, Budd McEntee, and my colleagues at WAGA-TV; my mother-in-law, Phyliss Reiman; my parents, who gave me the impetus to write; and my publisher, Chuck Perry, and his family.

Special thanks to Dr. Authur Cohen, one of America's preeminent psychologists, whose encouragement and vast knowledge made this book possible, and to his wife, Lois.

Introduction

———— ◄o► ————

Words have the power to create or destroy a child's spirit.

With encouraging words and genuine love, you can help your child blossom into a confident, happy adult who feels worthy of all the treasures life has to offer and who is sure to one day return the love received.

Words from a parent or caretaker can minimize a child's earliest fears and lay the foundation for a healthy sense of self later and a view of the world as a safe place where every dream becomes possible to achieve.

There is no greater gift an adult can give a child because there is nothing more empowering than the positive belief in one's self.

As a child you loved to hear these words; as an adult you will love to say them.

What better way for a child to start out in life!

Every Child Must Hear

— ◆ —

*S*elf-esteem begins in the cradle. Psychologists agree that even for the youngest child, language wields tremendous power. Infants will associate the words you use when addressing their primary needs with safety, comfort and love long after they are physically dependent. Caring words combined with body language and actions to match can nourish even the youngest human heart. Words can help a newborn establish a positive sense of self—an impression that can last a lifetime.

Children not only hear the words you use; they feel them.

You deserved to be born.

❧

You're a great baby!

——— ◄o► ———

I've looked forward to becoming
your mother/father.

❧

The world is a better place
because you are here.

We've been making special
preparations for your arrival.

⌒⌒

You were very brave and worked
very hard to get here.

⌒⌒

I'm so excited that you have
become part of my life.

You are a symbol of all hope.
Your birth gives the world a chance
for a new beginning.

∽

I'm pleased you were born a
girl/boy. I would love you regardless
of your gender.

∽

There is no one else like you in the
whole world.

ALDEN

You are safe here.

&

I want you to live.

—◄o►—

I enjoy spending time with you.
Your presence makes my
universe complete.

&

I'm so glad you are my child.

I need you as much as you
need me.

❧

You belong here. This is your home.

—◆—

I will always love you.

❧

You are important.

I want the best for you.

You are always good enough.

I will never leave you behind.

You've made a wonderful and
significant difference in my life.

I enjoy watching you grow.

❧

Take as much time as you need.
I'll be patient with you.

❧

You are strong and healthy.

I enjoy feeding you.

Kissing you is fun!

I loved being pregnant with you.

You can crawl when you are ready;
you can walk when you are ready;
you can talk when you are ready.

It's safe to explore. There's no limit to what you can achieve.

❧

You are destined for greatness.

◄◆►

It's possible to become whatever you choose.

❧

I'm here to support you.

your infant must hear

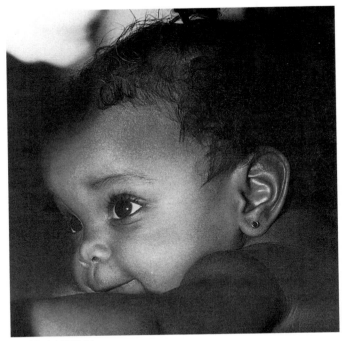

ALEXANDRIA ⟋

You will always be my daughter/son. I wouldn't give you up for all the tea in China.

❧

I won't ignore you. You deserve plenty of recognition and attention.

❧

I will hold you when you want me to. You deserve to be treated gently and with kindness.

I want you to feel good about yourself.

∽

I'm committed to you.

—◄○►—

You are lovable and huggable.

∽

You are naturally likeable.

You are smart.

∾

You mean everything to me.

——— ◄o► ———

You are the sweetness in my life.

∾

I won't use you to fill voids in
my life.

You make my life richer.

✐

I want you to be happy.

◄◆►

You are so special.

✐

You have my approval.

I'm so glad you are alive.

≈

You are a miracle.

— ◄◊► —

You are a wonderful person.

≈

I am taking very good care of you.

I enjoy rocking and cuddling you.

I have plenty of time and energy
to nurture you.

It's my delight to comfort and
reassure you. I won't ever leave
you for very long.

I won't make promises I can't keep.

I'm always available to you.

It's not your job to make other people happy. It's your job to play!

You are fine exactly as you are.

I'm glad you're a baby.

My life is better because you
are here.

You can count on me to make
sure your emotional and physical
needs are met.

MIRANDA

I'll take care of my needs so I can
take care of yours.

I wanted you to be born.

You are a priceless gift.

I'm lucky to share this life
with you.

You are capable of loving others.

❧

You contribute so much to our
family. Your family needs you.

———— ◄○► ————

Your home is a safe place filled
with love and kindness.

❧

I'll protect you from danger.

You don't have to be quiet to
be good.

∽

I'm not perfect. You don't have
to be, either.

∽

You are powerful and filled
with potential.

You are your own person.

∼◦∼

You were born creative and
imaginative.

—— ◄◦► ——

You radiate energy and light.

∼◦∼

You are a vital part of the world.

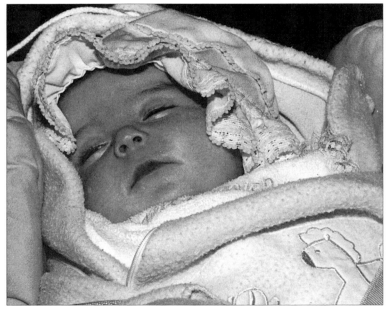

JANE MARGARET ✦

You are worthy of praise.

❧

You are worthy of being loved.

—◆—

I have an unlimited supply of
love to give you.

❧

You bring my life so much joy.

You are a great companion. You have so much to offer others.

The world is on your side. There are many people you can trust.

It's important to let others love you.

I appreciate you for just being you.

No one is of greater concern to me than you.

❦

I enjoy bathing you, brushing your hair and taking you for a stroll in the sunshine.

❦

You are worth sticking up for.

You are worthy of all the
treasures life has to offer.

You are valuable.

You are a blessing.

Your dreams can come true.

The world can be a marvelous place.

❧

You have all the resources you need
to have a wonderful life.

———— ❧ ————

You are needed, wanted and loved.

❧

God danced on the day you
were born.

your WORDS *toddler must hear*

———— ◄○► ————

In addition to the encouraging sentences already listed, toddlers need to hear words like "I think I can, I think I can." THE LITTLE ENGINE THAT COULD is more than a popular children's book; for many of us it contains the first affirmations we ever heard.

Such expressions help children realize they can succeed, that they'll be protected from strangers and strange objects, secure from day to night. Toddlers who learn they'll be loved regardless of their fears, feelings or moods "can" ultimately achieve just about anything.

You are worthy of my love just because you exist.

I'm glad you are you.

You're loved just as you are.

Your happiness is my top priority.

Your interests matter to me.

I enjoy laughing with you.

I love loving you.

I think about you all the time.

Your fears are not silly.

It's safe to tell me what's
bothering you. I'll help you
solve your problems.

I care about what you think and
how you feel. You are always
entitled to your own feelings.

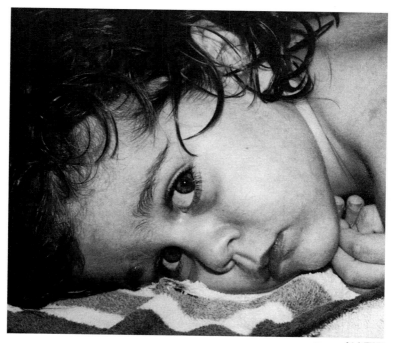

KATIE

37

It's okay to be afraid and vulnerable.

❧

It's okay to cry.

❧

You are free to experience rage, loneliness, envy, and other emotions. I'll never scold you for your feelings.

Everyone feels this way
sometimes.

∽

Let's talk about things that
bother you.

∽

It's okay to have feelings that are
different from mine.

You are a separate person and that's great.

෴

I cherish you for the qualities that make you unique.

෴

It's okay to think for yourself. You have options and choices.

You are an individual with your own timing for growth and development.

೧

You don't have to hurry. This is your time to be a child.

೧

I'm glad you are playful.

It's fun to pretend and play games.
This teaches you how to live in
the world.

You help me to be the free-spirited
child I was once.

Go ahead—day dream!

I would never do anything to crush your spontaneity.

You do so many things just right. You have many good qualities.

I learn so much from you.

I enjoy talking with you.

COLE ∾

I'll help you set boundaries and find balance in your life.

Mistakes are good; they help you learn.

It is okay to fail.

I won't make you jealous.

I won't embarrass you in front of others.

❧

I will listen without criticizing or judging you.

❧

It's okay to squirm, talk funny and be noisy in some places.

It's great to express yourself
freely and loudly.

∽

I want you to be heard as well
as seen.

∽

It's okay to be messy
sometimes.

You are more important than a
clean house.

❧

It's okay to be feminine.

———◆———

It's okay to be masculine.

❧

I love you exactly as you are today.

I see you!

You don't have to live up to
anyone's idea of a "model" child.

You don't have to act cute
to be loved.

It's okay to be cranky and tired.

You don't have to entertain me to get my attention.

∽

You don't have to earn my love.

——— ◄o► ———

You are safe, even when it's dark.

∽

I won't hurt you or abuse you.

If you do something wrong I might get angry; but I won't love you any less.

⤳⤶

You always are lovable, even when your behavior is not acceptable.

⤳⤶

I'll try to set clear and consistent standards for your behavior.

I know sometimes you behave the way you do not to defy me but to meet your own needs.

While I may put limits on your actions, I won't put limits on your feelings.

Pay attention to your feelings.

GRADY

I'll try to be honest with you about my feelings and take responsibility for them.

❧

I won't take my bad moods out on you.

❧

You deserve to be treated with respect.

You are entitled to have joy in
your life.

❧

It's a pleasure to hold you,
to feed you, to care for you and
to play with you.

❧

I admire you.

I trust you.

I take you seriously.

Needing others is a sign of strength.

I approve of the way you are.

I love all of you.

People will help you; all you
have to do is ask.

I have faith in your abilities.

It's important to ask for what you
want. Speak up for yourself.

I'm glad you're growing and learning.

∽

It's good that you're so curious.

——— ◄o► ———

It's good to taste and touch things.

∽

You can trust your intuition.

You can decide some things
for yourself: You can choose your
own friends, select the activities
you enjoy, and pick what you'd
like to wear.

❧

You can choose to feel good about
yourself.

❧

I value your input.

ELIZA & HELEN ✺

I'll help you whenever you need me to. You can count on me.

∽

I'll give you room to be independent.

——— ◆ ———

I will never abandon you.

∽

What can I do to help you feel safe?

I'm here to encourage you.

❧

You can do it.

——◆——

You did it!

❧

Bravo!

You are not the cause of any trouble in our relationship.

∽

You are not responsible for other people's problems.

◄○►

You are a good person.

∽

How about a hug!

A kiss before you go?

∽

I love you more every day. I know you love me, too.

∽

If people could look inside my heart, they'd see your face.

your school-age child must hear

WORDS

———— ◄◦► ————

As your children grow, so does the list of phrases they must hear. These words will give school-age children special encouragement. After all, this is a time of lions, tigers and bears. Oh my!

Your comforting words can help your child confront and overcome fears of thunder and lightning, witches and warlocks, monsters and creepy-crawly things.

Soothing words can help children deal with fears of sleeping alone and getting hurt, and with anxiety about their physical appearance and successful adjustment at school.

Words that communicate empathy and support can teach children invaluable lessons about their own strengths and about an adult's unwavering love.

I'm proud to be your mother/father.

You don't have to prove yourself
constantly to be loved.

I take great pleasure in you.

You're the best.

You do not need to take care of me; I will take care of you, because I am the adult and you are the child.

❧

Tell me about your goals, your hopes, your dreams.

❧

Tell me what scares you.

I may not like the way you behave sometimes, but I always love you.

⁓

You are never a "bad" person.

⁓

I'll make time to really listen to you.

You are the music in my life.

❧

I'll always let you know where
I am going and when I will return.

—— ◆ ——

I'll tell you what you can expect
to happen.

❧

I'll never desert you.

Show the world who you
really are.

❧

It's okay to bang pots and pans
sometimes.

❧

It's healthy to wonder and ask
questions.

NAOMI

Tell me what makes you sad.

I understand and accept what you
are feeling.

It's safe to express your feelings
and opinions.

I'm listening.

I'm watching.

❧

You make me so happy.

— ◄○► —

I appreciate your help.

❧

You can make an important
difference in the world.

All is well at home.

❧

It's okay to have your friends over.

⸺ ❖ ⸺

I couldn't have done it better
myself.

❧

I'll pay attention to your
verbal and nonverbal messages.

It's okay to be self-absorbed sometimes. I know it's part of your development.

❧

I'll try not to lose my temper.

❧

I won't blame you for any of the decisions I make.

I won't always give in to you.

When you do something wrong,
I'll try to understand.

I won't say or do things that
might make you feel ashamed or
humiliated.

your school-age child must hear WORDS

ERIC & SCOTT

I'll laugh with you, never at you.

〜

You have control over your actions.

━━ ◄○► ━━

If you didn't do it, it's not your fault.

〜

Children don't cause divorces,
parents do.

You are entitled to your own ideas.

There is more than one right answer.

You don't have to get a perfect report card.

You don't have to do equally well in all subjects.

It's alright to learn in your own way.

Everyone makes mistakes.

You'll do better next time.

You will improve with practice.

I appreciate your effort.

You did your best and that's good enough.

I want you to learn in a nurturing, low-pressure environment.

I know you're working really hard.

You're heading in the right direction.

You are capable and strong.

You are a winner.

You are already a success!

I'll try not to set up unrealistic expectations of you.

❧

While you may do some things that disappoint me, you as a person are never a disappointment.

❧

You won't lose my love.

You don't have to eat everything
on your plate.

೧ ೨

You don't have to always act
your age.

೧ ೨

I understand you're developing
at your own speed.

You are responsible for making some decisions.

∽

You get to decide which toys you want to share and when and with whom.

∽

You make good choices.

It's okay to be assertive.

❧

You can stand up for yourself.

❧

I realize that sometimes when
you disobey me you are just testing
your separateness, proving
your realness.

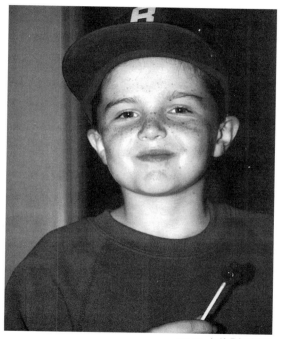

≈ MICHAEL

I'll try to see the world from your perspective.

❧

I won't embarrass you by correcting you in front of others.

—◄○►—

I cherish you.

❧

You're doing a great job!

WORDS

I'm proud of the way you behaved today.

❧

You have so many strengths. Let's list them.

◆

Excellent!

❧

You are learning so fast!

Recognize your own magnificence.

I value you apart from your achievements.

I love your freckles, your curly hair, your soft skin. I love your smile!

I love you no matter how you look.

I accept you as you are.

The real gift is who you are inside.

I love how clever you are.

You are an essential part
of our family. We all need
each other.

I'm glad you belong to us.

You are fun to be with.

I enjoy spending time with you
and playing with you.

I enjoy reading with you.

It's okay to be afraid of going to school. The adults will look after you.

❧

I won't demand more than you are capable of giving.

❧

Whenever you act on your behalf, I will support you.

DREW, CYNTHIA & DEREK

I have a terrific time teaching you.

⸙

School is a great place to learn
and make friends.

——— ◄○► ———

I'll stand in harm's way. I'll protect
you from adversity.

⸙

It's okay to be dependent.

I encourage you to be independent.

❧

It's okay to have secrets.

— ◆ —

I respect your privacy.

❧

I'll let you do it yourself if you want to.

WORDS

It's good to take risks and try new things.

❧

I love you when you are quiet and when you are wild.

❧

You can expect your parents to care for you and protect you.

No one has the right to hurt you.

∽∽

There is no one I love more
than you.

—◄o►—

There's enough love in this
family for everyone.

∽∽

It's great to care about others.

When you grow up you can have your own career and have a family.

∽

Your home can be a sweet, safe place.

—◄◦►—

You can be in love forever.

∽

You can have the job you've always dreamed of.

It's possible to have close, caring friends.

∽

It's possible to have a wonderful marriage.

◄○►

It's possible to have inner peace.

∽

It's possible to be happy and to have a wonderful life.

It is not necessary to use every phrase or to communicate these words with any particular frequency.

The objective is to help children foster good feelings about themselves and the world.

You can even come up with your own words your child must hear. That's what this space is for:

....

....

....

....

....

....

....

....

every parent should read BOOKS

◄◦►

Bloch, D. POSITIVE SELF-TALK FOR CHILDREN. New York: Bantam books, 1993.

Corkille, B. YOUR CHILD'S SELF-ESTEEM. New York: Doubleday, 1970.

Curry, N., and C. Johnson. BEYOND SELF-ESTEEM. Washington, D.C.: National Association for the Education of Young Children, 1980.

Garber, S., M. Garber, and R. Freedman. MONSTERS UNDER THE BED AND OTHER CHILDHOOD FEARS. New York: Villard Books, 1993.

Greenberg, P. CHARACTER DEVELOPMENT: ENCOURAGING SELF-ESTEEM AND SELF-DISCIPLINE. Washington, D.C.: National Association for the Education of Young Children, 1991.

Hay, L. YOU CAN HEAL YOUR LIFE. Hay House, 1984.

Kaufman, G., and L. Raphael. STICK UP FOR YOURSELF. Free Spirit Publishing, 1990.

Kutner, L. PARENT AND CHILD. New York: William Morrow, 1991.

Leach, P. BABYHOOD. New York: Alfred A. Knopf, 1993.

every parent should read BOOKS

Lerner, R. AFFIRMATIONS FOR THE INNER CHILD. Heath Communications, 1990.

Miller, A. THE DRAMA OF THE GIFTED CHILD. New York: Basic Books, 1981.

Peck, S. THE ROAD LESS TRAVELED. New York: Simon and Schuster, 1978.

Salk, L. FAMILYHOOD. New York: Simon and Schuster, 1992.

Share your words with the author:
Cynthia Good
WAGA-TV
1551 Briarcliff Road
Atlanta, GA 30306